Solace

Empowering Pastors' Wives to Prevent and Overcome Burnout

Patricia Aladekoba, Ed.D

SOLACE:
EMPOWERING PASTORS' WIVES TO PREVENT AND OVERCOME BURNOUT

Published by Paradise Restored Publishing
Owings Mills, Maryland, United States of America

Copyright © 2024 Patricia Aladekoba
Edited by Morenike Euba Oyenusi
Book design by Streetlight Graphics, LLC

First edition 2024

The information contained in this book is for educational purposes only. The author and publisher are not engaged in rendering medical or other professional advice. If such advice is needed, the services of a qualified professional should be sought. The views expressed in this book are those of the author and do not necessarily reflect the views of the publisher.

All rights reserved. No part of this book may be reproduced, distributed, transmitted, stored, or used in any manner, form, or by any means, including photocopying, recording, or other electronic or mechanical means, without prior written permission from the copyright owner, except for the use of brief quotations embodied in a book review and certain other noncommercial uses permitted by copyright law.

All emphases in Scripture quotations and other quotations are the author's, unless otherwise specified. Scriptures quoted are taken from the King James Version of the Bible, public domain, unless otherwise specified.

Publisher's Cataloging-in-Publication Data provided by Five Rainbows Cataloging Services
Names: Aladekoba, Patricia, author.
Title: Solace : empowering pastors' wives to prevent and overcome burnout / Patricia Aladekoba, Ed. D.
Description: First edition. | Owings Mills, MD : Paradise Restored Publishing, 2024. | Includes bibliographical references.
Identifiers: LCCN 2024903570 (print) | ISBN 978-1-953685-13-1 (hardcover : dust jacket) | ISBN 978-1-953685-14-8 (hardcover) | ISBN 978-1-953685-15-5 (paperback) | ISBN 978-1-953685-16-2 (ebook)
Subjects: LCSH: Spouses of clergy--United States--Religious life. | Christian women--United States--Religious life. | Wives--Religious life. | Pastoral care. | Burn out (Psychology)--Religious aspects--Christianity. | BISAC: RELIGION / Christian Living / Women's Interests. | RELIGION / Christian Church / Administration. | RELIGION / Christian Living / Family & Relationships. | RELIGION / Christian Ministry / Pastoral Resources.
Classification: LCC BV4395 .A43 2024 (print) | LCC BV4395 (ebook) | DDC 253/.22--dc23.

Dr. Patricia Aladekoba
paladekoba@yahoo.com
pat_tricius
@patricia.aladekoba
@tricius5

Paradise Restored Publishing
info@paradiserestoredpublishing.com
www.paradiserestoredpublishing.com
@morenikeeubaoyenusi
@paradiserestoredpublishing
@morenikeeubaoyenusi

Paradise on earth…through a good book! ™

Printed in the United States of America

Table of Contents

Dedication 1

Foreword 3

Chapter One: Introduction 7

Chapter Two: The Pastor's Marriage 19

Chapter Three: Roles of Pastors' Wives 25

Chapter Four: Sources of Stress 35

Chapter Five: Coping Strategies 41

Chapter Six: Spiritual Distortions About
the Work of Ministry 45

Chapter Seven: Recommendations 53

Chapter Eight: Conclusion 57

Appendix A ... 63
   A Poem for the Pastor's Wife ... 65
   A Bill of Rights for the Pastor's Wife ... 67

Bibliography ... 71

Acknowledgements ... 75

About the Author ... 77

Dedication

I dedicate this book to pastors' wives all over the world. As the church of Jesus Christ continues to grow around the globe, this book will reshape the way pastors' wives and their families are viewed in ministry, and it will guide pastors, the church leadership, counselors, psychologists, and other stakeholders in the right direction as they seek to provide help to pastors' wives.

Foreword

THE ROLE OF A PASTOR'S wife carries unique demands and pressures that can take a heavy toll. Though the specifics vary in different church contexts, most pastors' wives are expected to be actively engaged in ministry while also managing the duties of home and family. It is a calling that requires great sacrifice of time, energy, and personal needs.

I had the honor and privilege of co-supervising Dr. Patricia Aladekoba's dissertation work on this important topic and hooding her at her graduation ceremony. Her personal experience as a pastor's wife in the African Pentecostal Church led her to want to study this phenomenon. In this important book, Dr. Aladekoba explores the rising problem of burnout among pastors' wives. Drawing on extensive research and interviews, she gives voice to the exhaustion, isolation, and sense of duty that many of these women grapple with. Dr. Aladekoba's book makes it abundantly clear that we need to re-evaluate expectations placed on pastors' wives and provide better structures of care and support. Some of the highlighted themes in this seminal work include protective factors such as self-care, financial strains, isolation, and lack of boundaries.

Burnout in ministry is never simply a personal failure. It points to flaws in systems that allow unrealistic workloads, lack of work-life balance, and failure to prioritize self-care. Through compelling storytelling and insightful analysis, Dr. Aladekoba makes the case that preventing burnout among pastors' wives is a responsibility churches must prioritize. Care for the caregiver is essential for sustainable and healthy church communities.

I am so proud of my former student, Dr. Patricia Aladekoba. Her heart for pastors' wives led her to create this essential piece of work that will no doubt help so many people. I hope this book sparks needed conversations in congregations about enacting change. Pastors' wives deserve understanding, boundaries, and spiritual and emotional support from those they serve. My prayer is that these pages challenge all of us to do better in caring for the women who give so much of themselves in their ministry callings. The time for awareness, compassion and action is now.

Dr. Krystal L. Clemons
Professor of Counseling, Denver Seminary
Founder & CEO, Clemons Education Consulting LLC

"BURNOUT" IS THE "EXTINCTION OF MOTIVATION OR INCENTIVE, ESPECIALLY WHERE ONE'S DEVOTION TO A CAUSE OR RELATIONSHIP FAILS TO PRODUCE THE DESIRED RESULTS."

Chapter One
INTRODUCTION

FOR MANY YEARS, PASTORS' WIVES have been experiencing and continue to experience burnout. One may wonder why. The pastorate of a church is for godly men and women called by God into such a high position. However, there are so many stressors that have led to pastors' wives suffering from burnout[1]. The work of ministry can become so demanding not just to the minister but to his wife as well. I know firsthand about this experience. I am a pastor's wife.

The term "burnout" is a relatively new term, first coined in 1974 by Herbert Freudenberger, a German-born American psychologist. He originally described "burnout" as the "extinction of motivation or incentive, especially where one's devotion to a cause or relationship fails to produce the desired results" (p.63). Observing the physical, mental, and emotional toll that working in a public service arena can take on staff and volunteers, Freudenberger's phenomenon of "burnout" could not

---

1   Burnout is not limited to pastors' wives alone. The husbands of female pastors and ministers are also susceptible to burnout. However, in this book, I have chosen to focus on the wives of male pastors and ministers.

have been more appropriate. The term is now used loosely in discussions of stress, especially in job-related situations. Sadly, men and women leaders in the church also experience burnout in their vocational group just like other service professions.

Through extensive research, I have been led to conclude that there has been very little done to help pastors' wives overcome the stresses that come with the job. Even the churches where they serve have not provided pastoral care or counseling to help them. In thinking about the duties and demands of a pastor, people often forget what a heavy load the pastor's wife is carrying. She is often swept into the shadows as the pastor is elevated as the only one who needs mentoring, training, and direction. Pastors' wives are very much in need of such mentoring as well. Programs should be developed even within the church to help pastors' wives deal with some of the stressors of ministry work and family life that can lead to burnout and its accompanying symptoms.

My Faith Tradition

Before discussing my personal journey as a pastor's wife, I would like first to talk about my faith tradition which I believe has been the basis of my spirituality.

I was born and raised in Freetown, a city in Sierra Leone in West Africa. I would say that I found myself privileged to have been born in a home where the utmost priority was placed not just on education, but also on Christian living and one's relationship with the Lord. I can say in no uncertain terms that I accepted Jesus as my personal Savior at the young age of 13 while in high school. I became a member of my school's society of Christian youths. I was fully devoted to this, and I always found happiness being in the company of fellow believers.

My love for the Lord and dedication to the things of God, I believe, stemmed from the fact that not only did our parents instill Christian values in me, but I grew up in a family where my grandparents and some of my uncles from the maternal side of my family were Anglican pastors. Suffice it to say that this became the bedrock for my strong Christian faith. My siblings and I were raised as orthodox Christians. We could recite the Psalms and sing hymns; we knew various Bible scriptures, and the like. I went through the Christian rituals, of baptism when I was an infant, and then confirmation, in which I was allowed to partake of the Holy Communion, as a teenager. I went to church every Sunday with my parents and participated in various church activities as a child.

Beginning from my college years, I have tried my best truly to follow the dictates of our Lord and Savior. I have stayed on the path of the Lord. I work ceaselessly for God. Now firmly in adulthood, I am in church as often as I can. I pray even more fervently. I read the Bible more frequently and have daily devotions, sometimes in quiet meditation. I have always loved the Lord ardently and have tried wholeheartedly to walk in His path. However, I became drawn to the Pentecostal way of worship because I was more in tune with the presence of the Holy Spirit than when I attended an orthodox service at an Anglican church, for example. In addition, in the Pentecostal Church, a significant amount of time is allotted for praise and worship and 'fellowshipping' afterwards, all of which I really relish.

I became a member of one of the Pentecostal churches and was a part of the praise and worship team. Serving the Lord has always been paramount in my life, and I did just that. I also served in other departments within the church, and I found comfort and happiness doing so. Little did I know that the Lord was preparing me for something greater. So, many years down the road when I became a pastor's wife, I thought that it was going to be an easy task, since I had been used to holding various positions in the church and assisting men and women of God in ministry.

I found out that being a pastor's wife requires a lot of grace and patience. Let me provide an example. My husband, Tony, was at one time the Senior Pastor of Christ Apostolic Church (World Soul-Winning Evangelistic Ministry), a Pentecostal church. In this church, there was a strong Nigerian influence.

The members often spoke Yoruba, one of the Nigerian languages, which was isolating for those who do not speak the language. Vain and ceaseless efforts to educate the Nigerian members not to speak their native language and to be sensitive to the presence of members and visitors of other nationalities, some first-time church attendees, was a source of stress and frustration for me. My husband, who is Nigerian, expressed similar concerns. This is but one example of concerns which led to my becoming stressed as the wife of a pastor. In the next few chapters, I discuss the issue of unrealistic expectations and subsequent burnout among pastors' wives in more detail as well as examine the theological and spiritual aspects of burnout.

My Personal Journey

Some people may wonder how it was that I became a pastor's wife. Was it a divine ordination? Did I happen to fall in love with a man who was a minister of God? I believe the answer to each of these questions is a resounding "yes!" Others may still ask, "But, how did it all happen?" How did it happen? I got married to a man who later became a pastor, after I had had a failed relationship. I was devastated and depressed, and I cried out to the Lord for a man of God. God answered my prayers and blessed me with one!

Let me hasten to say that when we got married, he was the man of my dreams. He was not a pastor, then. He was the man of God I truly desired. We prayed together, we went to the house of God together, we spent a whole lot of time together; we pretty much did everything together. To me that is what makes for a good family. Life was fun, interesting, happy, and I felt privileged to be married to a man of God. The disappointment I had experienced a year or so ago in my previous relationship was now like a dream. I thought to myself, "God is good!"

About a year later, we became members of another ministry. Here, my husband continued his duties faithfully as a

> I was devastated and depressed, and I cried out to the Lord for a man of God. God answered my prayers and blessed me with one!

servant of God. After a few months, he was ordained an evangelist. Family life was still the same, but he now had duties assigned to him by the church. He would sometimes accompany the Senior Pastor of the church on hospital or home visits to members of the congregation. He spent more time in church either for prayer or for counseling sessions. But he still made time for family and all other family-related activities.

In a year, he was ordained a pastor and assigned to head one of the churches within the ministry. We were both excited about the successive promotions and we prayed and thanked God for them. He was now the Senior Pastor of that church since the pastor there had been transferred to another church. Accordingly, my husband assumed full leadership of the church. He became so engrossed in making sure that the work he had been assigned did not fall through the cracks. There were a lot of 'gaps' within the church, both administratively and spiritually. And my husband, being the devoted man of God that he is, wanted to 'fix' it all! Even though I was thrilled about the new opportunity, I was a little apprehensive about the future. I saw that my husband, who had always had time for the family and doing things with the family–praying, being with our then newborn son–had now to spend hours on end in church. He always had to meet with some department head or try to resolve age-old conflicts amongst family members or members of the church, or to organize some prayer meeting so that the church could be awakened spiritually. I saw the man of God that I had once cherished being swept away by the cares and burdens of other people. I saw myself losing my husband to the work of ministry.

At the time of his appointment, I became full of anticipation, having no idea what lay ahead of us. I saw our future through rose-colored glasses. My heart of innocence knew nothing of the mountains and valleys that lay before us. One of my greatest joys had been to labor side by side in ministry with my husband and to know that we were on the same team. But as days and months went by, it seemed as if I was being

> I saw the man of God that I had once cherished being swept away by the cares and burdens of other people. I saw myself losing my husband to the work of ministry.

moved from the position that I had always anticipated. My husband was so enmeshed in all those activities of the church that I rarely saw him. I tried to caution him at times that he could only do but so much. However, his response was always, "Honey, we cannot fail God!"

I began feeling exhausted. I was working full time, with two young kids at the time, both under four, going to graduate school, and I was still expected by my husband and even the parishioners to be in church for every activity–in addition to Sunday service, there was a "share and care" program on Tuesdays, Bible study on Wednesdays, and night vigils on Fridays. So, there were these unrealistic expectations of the pastor, his wife, and their family. My conviction was that no matter how hard we tried, we could not meet everyone's expectations as each person is different. We could only be true to the call that God had placed on our lives. We constantly had to remind ourselves to play to an audience of One, namely God Himself.

Not only was I going through stressful situations, but I also became very lonely. Loneliness is one of the symptoms of burnout. The man I used to spend almost all my time with, pray with, talk and laugh with, was now more concerned about his flock and tending to them, than with the wife God had given him. He expressed as his main concern that he did not want to be held accountable by God if his flock strayed, and he believed his wife would always be there for him and stick with him no matter what. However, he did not realize that I felt abandoned and burdened, not just by his expectations, but by those of the congregation as well. To make matters more difficult, I am from Sierra Leone and my husband is from Nigeria. I cannot speak any of the Nigerian languages, so you can imagine how alone I felt when people of his ethnicity would just walk up to talk to him and start speaking in their language, oblivious of or ignoring the fact that I do not speak nor understand the language. Thank God for His grace!

...BECAUSE OF PEOPLE'S UNREALISTIC EXPECTATIONS OF ME, I BEGAN TO EXPERIENCE BURNOUT AND A DEEP SENSE OF LONELINESS. THE DEMANDS OF FAMILY LIFE WERE BECOMING TOO MUCH AS WELL.

The Pastor's Wife

I never bargained for what this position demanded. However, knowing that I was born into a lineage that had a slew of pastors, I believe that it did not happen by chance. This was not a role I had sought to have in life. I simply fell in love with a man who was called into ministry. Initially, my husband and I were excited about our new "roles", and we could see the immense potential there was in the Kingdom of God. We planned on serving God well; we wanted to sow into the Kingdom; we wanted to live the adventure; we wanted to make God proud. Faithfully, we went where the Lord led us. But because of people's unrealistic expectations of me, I began to experience burnout and a deep sense of loneliness. The demands of family life were becoming too much as well.

Research validates my observation that there are many pastors' wives out there who have experienced and continue to experience burnout and loneliness. Some have thrown in the towel because they could not take it any longer. Others have hung in there because they believe that it is their calling, tough as it might be. I am staying the course because I believe that it was the Lord's desire for me to be married to a man of God. I always remind myself that "… the joy of the Lord is my strength." (Nehemiah 8: 10).

My husband continues to help me understand the struggles that come with ministry work and has taken great strides over the years in readjusting his schedules. There are times when he sends me flowers and takes me out to dinner to show appreciation to me for being there for and with him. When we go to minister in other churches, he acknowledges me and asks for a round of applause for his "lovely wife", who not only takes care of the children when he goes away, but who stands by him and supports him in ministry. Those are always special moments for me because, no matter how emotionally exhausted I am feeling at the time, his words light up my spirit.

...HE ACKNOWLEDGES ME AND ASKS FOR A ROUND OF APPLAUSE FOR HIS "LOVELY WIFE", WHO NOT ONLY TAKES CARE OF THE CHILDREN WHEN HE GOES AWAY, BUT WHO STANDS BY HIM AND SUPPORTS HIM IN MINISTRY. THOSE ARE ALWAYS SPECIAL MOMENTS FOR ME BECAUSE, NO MATTER HOW EMOTIONALLY EXHAUSTED I AM FEELING AT THE TIME, HIS WORDS LIGHT UP MY SPIRIT.

...BECAUSE HE AND HIS WIFE ARE LIVING IN A FISHBOWL, THEIR MARRIAGE AND FAMILY LIFE ARE USUALLY ON DISPLAY FOR EVERYONE TO FIXATE UPON.

Chapter Two
The Pastor's Marriage

THE MARRIAGE OF THE PASTOR and his wife can be a teaching example to members of his congregation about love and having a good and strong marriage that will be an asset to their ministry. Does that mean that the pastor's marriage will be ideal or perfect? No! But because he and his wife are living in a fishbowl, their marriage and family life are usually on display for everyone to fixate upon. If the pastor is to have a successful ministry, it is vital that the churches that he leads and the congregations that he shepherds understand the connection between a happy marriage and a successful ministry and the stresses that can have a devastating effect on his marriage. Churches need to be sensitized to the fact that if their church is going to remain healthy and stay vibrant, the health of the pastor's marriage is a key component to the success and well-being of the church.

Psychologist, Diane Langberg, believes that marriage and ministry should fit together:

> ...THE HEALTH OF THE PASTOR'S MARRIAGE IS A KEY COMPONENT TO THE SUCCESS AND WELL-BEING OF THE CHURCH.

Many couples believe and live as if marriage and ministry do not fit together. They view these two areas as being in irresolvable conflict and feel that one must be subordinate. Frequently, this translates into a severe neglect of the family, because 'serving the Lord' is more important. Those having this attitude define service to God as 'those spiritual things that take place outside the home' (Langberg, p. 7).

The problem here is that many couples do not see how ministry and marriage are interconnected. Many pastors do not see the connection of the ministry to their marriage. The pastor's wife is not just the helpmeet to her husband (Beeke, 2013). If the pastor neglects his ministry in the home, it cannot only be detrimental to the spouse but also to the children.

Pastors and their spouses should be able to show the interconnectedness of their marriage and ministry so that the former can serve as an example to singles in the church who are looking to get married someday. This will enable marriage to be a desirable standard for all young people (Comiskey, 2022). The institution was created by God for procreation, dominion, and companionship. It is the minister's obligation to reawaken the consciousness that marriage is still a God-created institution open to all who desire to be married.

A pastor's marriage should also provide healthy relationship growth and stability for developing children. The presence of both parents in the home is important in the development of the children's moral code and the parents in turn become role models for their growing children (Comiskey, 2022). This can make for a successful ministry and marriage. These facts are learned when couples, pastors and their spouses included, go through premarital counseling before marriage.

The Cost of Caring for the Caregiver

The pastor is always at the forefront helping church members with their emotional and spiritual growth (Chan & Wong, 2018). Pastoral work can become very stressful, not just in the Pentecostal denominations, but also in all other non-charismatic ones. Pastors can become very busy as they attend to the needs of their congregations which can result in physical and emotional exhaustion. When pastors are drained and unable to cope with the stresses that come with their profession, it not only affects them, but it also takes on the wife and the children (Chan & Chen, 2019). This brings the question to play, "Who cares for the clergy and his family in times of stress and emotional exhaustion?"

A pastor's wife faces distinct challenges as the wife of a man with a high profile and demanding job (Luedtke & Sneed, 2018). As a result, because of the nature of their positions, roles, and backgrounds, pastors' wives cannot be neglected or excluded. Pastors' wives desire for their needs and experiences to be understood. According to Luedtke and Sneed (2018), "their lived experience comprises positive and negative components and brings mental, emotional, spiritual, and physical awareness to onlookers" (p. 69). The contributions of Luedtke and Sneed have led to the understanding of the struggles and rewards women face daily and for those pastors' wives, who may be suffering silently.

When talking about the pastor's wife's position in her husband's ministry, the word "helpmeet" comes up frequently. While this phrase may appear outdated and out of touch with today's culture, it is truly a wonderful word that God gave to describe the bond between a lady and her husband. The ministry to her spouse is the one ministry that a pastor's wife should have. She must support and encourage her husband for him to succeed. There is no better assurance a wife can provide to her husband than knowing that she is rooting for him and believes in him (Beeke, 2011). He needs to feel that someone is on his side because the pressures of ministry can be overpowering at times. That is why she must be his cheerleader and protector.

Women must realize that marriage is about a relationship, and that relationships develop and expand with time. There will be occasions when the pastor and his wife disagree on important subjects. However, it is during these moments that they must learn to protect and care for their marriage and each other. They must also learn to communicate with each other, to become closest friends, to support each other, and to create mutual trust. Their home should be a relaxing and peaceful environment for them both. They must learn how to safeguard and guard their residence (Armstrong, 2013).

> As the emotional demands on pastors' wives increase, it is important to consider their assumed roles.

Chapter Three
Roles of Pastors' Wives

As the emotional demands on pastors' wives increase, it is important to consider their assumed roles. The pastor usually has prescribed roles and job specifications unlike the pastor's wife who does not. Beeke (2013) stated that the wife of a pastor has a high calling. Her calling as his wife engages her in special responsibilities and special honor. The pastor's wife is a woman worthy of honor. She can be likened to the woman described in Proverbs 31: 30, "a woman that feareth the Lord". She is a godly woman.

Empirical research and meta-studies addressing the roles of clergy[2] spouses, such as those conducted by Drumm, *et al.* (2017), reveal that wives see the job as multi-layered. It entails spiritually, emotionally, physically, and cognitively supporting her clergy husband, and it can be difficult, taxing, self-sacrificing, and emotionally draining (Andor, 2013). Andor mentions

---

[2] The terms "pastor" and "clergy" are used interchangeably.

> ...THE JOB IS MULTI-LAYERED. IT ENTAILS SPIRITUALLY, EMOTIONALLY, PHYSICALLY, AND COGNITIVELY SUPPORTING HER CLERGY HUSBAND, AND IT CAN BE DIFFICULT, TAXING, SELF-SACRIFICING, AND EMOTIONALLY DRAINING

the stress, loneliness, and isolation that may accompany the role of pastors' wives.

The study conducted by Guzman and Teh (2016) on Filipino clergy wives described the husband and father as the head of the church and home, and the wife as taking on multiple roles as her husband's support, house manager, and breadwinner as well. These participants did not have housekeepers at home, as is the practice in most Filipino families. Clergy wives had to compete with their husband's time. As a result of his ministry, he may not have been available or at home even during family emergencies, such as when the children were sick. Some of the working clergy wives had to sacrifice their time at work, and this usually brought about tension in their marital relationships.

Various types of stressors that accompany pastor spouses have been identified by researchers, writers, and journalists. Some of these stressors include but are not limited to the following: "boundary-related stress, role expectation/confusion, lack of time/time pressures, loneliness, lack of privacy/fishbowl effect, financial strain, lack of social support, and employment and educational challenges" (Drumm, *et al.*, 2017, p. 95). The presence and effects of these stressors related to the pastor's wife's role reveal the lack of a consistent description of the components defining the role itself. Some defining elements of the pastors' wives' roles include, but are not limited to, "(a) providing emotional support for the pastor (her spouse); (b) conforming to particular standards of appearance; (c) being capable in specific ways such as music, hospitality, career; (d) attending church events; (e) being an example to others; (f) keeping quiet; and (g) doing things like or being like the former pastor's spouse" (Drumm, *et al.*, 2017).

The stressors experienced by pastors' wives are often chronic and can negatively affect their physical, mental, spiritual, and overall wellbeing. Drumm, *et al.* (2017) posit that "lack of defining elements of what comprises role expectations leads not only to a mixed approach in measurement in related research, but on a more personal level for this population, reveals an issue that may have negative implications for pastors' spouses' emotional health and life satisfaction—the question of role ambiguity" (p. 95).

One's reading of the Bible without a doubt raises the question, "What does the Bible say about the nature of the work of the pastor's wife?" The Bible only implicitly addresses the issue and does not distinguish the role of the pastor's wife from the function of other women in the assembly. According to the notion of the two-person career, pastors' wives are believed to take on more roles than wives whose husbands work in other caring or helpful professions, such as medical professionals, paramedics, teachers, or social workers. In some church denominations, the woman is seen as an augmenting agent in her husband's ministry, and the ministry's success or failure is attributed to her (Litchfield, 2016). Many churches have traditionally required pastors' wives to be flexible, believers, decent wives, and mothers, according to Litchfield (2016). Ash (2011) suggests that roles are often gender-driven and include a variety of mediums within the church, such as being involved in children's activities, leading women's groups, counseling, assisting with parenting, visiting shut-ins, overseeing worship teams, managing the church's cleaning and internal decorations, such as flowers, and performing clerical tasks.

The ministerial responsibilities of a pastor's wife in the congregation are the same as those of any other woman in the congregation. Paul's advice to the aged women is that each should grow in godly character and cultivate a suitable relationship with her husband and children (Titus 2:3-5). She is to be encouraged to instruct the younger women in the assembly when it comes to teaching. However, the young pastor should regard his wife as a student of the elder women in the church before she qualifies as a teacher of adult women, according to Paul's exhortation.

The stability of the pastor's home is a necessary requirement for his ongoing ministry, and the pastor's wife is obviously a major contributor to that stability. The profound implications of the fact that her efforts in the home directly influence his capacities to lead the flock of God should be carefully considered. In her role as wife, her daily labors serve to maintain her husband's qualification to shepherd God's flock by helping him remain faithful as the shepherd of his home. According to Andor (2013), one of the few depictions from a black perspective, the pastor's wife's function is considered vital in the Seventh-day Adventist tradition. Wives are seen as an augmenting agent to their husbands' ministries in Ghana. Andor reaffirms the necessity of learning about the Pentecostal tradition's history and what it means to women in the tradition. Traditions and unwritten norms are sometimes seen as binding as scripture in church settings with a mostly black congregation, and if, as Andor (2013) proposes, the pastor's wife is an enhancing agent, what impact might this have on women in the church?

According to Miller (2009),

> Every pastoral couple wants to hear the accolade that the pastor's wife is a good pastor's wife. But there are ample false criteria upon which such a judgment is popularly based. Too often such status is conferred on the mere determination that she is a good listener, or a faithful friend to other women, an effective speaker, or a skilled musician, a stunning administrative organizer, or simply a woman who is really busy serving God (p. 1).

Miller, 2009, also has the following to say:

> On the authority of God's Word[3], a pastor's wife can be a good pastor's wife only insofar as she is a faithful helper to her husband, a diligent keeper of her home, a godly mother to her children, and a solid force in keeping her husband qualified for ministry by edifying his home. Though she teaches with the tongues of men and of angels, though she proves to be earth's very best friend, though she wins scores of souls to Christ, though she organizes one or more potluck dinners, if she is not a success as the God-given helper to her husband and mother to her children, she is not a good pastor's wife (p. 1).

Francis, *et al.* (2013) investigated the personality of the pastor and the impact it might have on the pastoral role experience. Andor (2013) explores this topic in the context of pastors' wives, claiming that the pastor's wife's personality can play a big influence in her adjusting, embracing, or disconnecting from the job (p. 28).

It is important to examine in more detail the expectations and assumptions held by pastors' wives' and by others of what the roles of pastors' wives should be as they work alongside their husbands in ministry, and the stresses of family life and ministry they are exposed to.

As I have discussed, the role of a pastor's wife is generally understood but not necessarily clearly defined. It is unclear what a new bride expects from a life of being married to a pastor. The demands made upon her depend upon a variety of factors, including her denomination, geographic location, and the size of her community, as well as her personal back-

---

3   For example, Proverbs 31:10-31.

ground and temperament. Pastors' wives come from various denominations and religious traditions, and they all face the demands that come with their position. Based on some of these traditions, it has always been clear that the role of women and children is not the same in the society as that of the father or the male. The mother is typically seen as being the opposite of the father: passive, and submissive. She is expected to listen and implement what she is told without any questions despite bearing most of the burden in the family. She is invisible and inferior. This belief is carried over even when she becomes a pastor's wife. The pastor's wife is usually not regarded as clergy or laity, and as such has no rights within the current church system. Aulthouse, 2013, Hester, 2018, and Luedtke & Sneed, 2018 have discovered that pastors' wives experience high levels of stress. The uncertainty of the role of a pastor's wife, for example, is a source of stress. Another cause of stress is how the congregation perceives and expects the pastor's spouse and children to be examples to others and be on their best behavior. (Hester, 2018). Pastors' spouses also indicate emotions of loneliness and anger have increased (Hester, 2018).

Hoffert (2019) opined that "the triple burden of carrying out their domestic duties as wives, mothers, and housekeepers, promoting efforts to encourage the search for personal salvation, and performing community service comes as a way of fulfilling the expectations imposed on them by their husbands' congregations" (p. 246). Because pastors' wives often tried to carry out these duties without adequate financial resources, some ministers' wives took on a fourth burden—that of co-breadwinner, which called upon them to teach school, take on sewing, sell produce, or keep a boarding house (Hoffert, 2019). Financial constraints within the pastors' families have led the wives to take up other job opportunities. Pastors' wives may not have anticipated the need to fulfill such roles. Some may not have embraced it so well.

What role should pastors' wives play in the church? There are job descriptions and expectations that many congregations have come to expect when they view the position of a pastor's wife (Armstrong, 2013; Guzman & Teh, 2016; Chan & Wong, 2018). When churches advertise for the position of a pastor, they do not include the position of a pastor's wife. They anticipate that when the pastor is hired, they will be getting a complete package that includes a wife that will work alongside her husband in the church, mostly without pay (Beeke, 2013). However, a pastor's wife should be no different from any other Christian woman in the church.

Pastors may be prepared for their role in the church, but some pastors' wives may not be as prepared. Some feel unqualified and discouraged about their position, especially from the responsibilities thrust upon them. Most pastors' wives believe that God will meet their needs and help them overcome any struggle in ministry. When such expectations do not become evident as quickly as they thought, they may begin to feel alienated, not only from God, but also from their husbands, and from those in their congregation that they believed loved and cared about them (Luedtke & Sneed, 2018).

When ministry demands become too overwhelming, the pastor's wife might become less effective in fulfilling her duties at home as a wife and as a mother. She may become discouraged and disillusioned, and her frustration may be taken out on her husband, if she believes he has allowed others to dictate her responsibilities within the ministry. The pastor's wife should be able to function like any other woman in the church with unique gifts and God-given abilities.

When ministry demands become too overwhelming, the pastor's wife might become less effective in fulfilling her duties at home as a wife and as a mother. She may become discouraged and disillusioned, and her frustration may be taken out on her husband, if she believes he has allowed others to dictate her responsibilities within the ministry.

> Pastoral stress is a growing phenomenon in all religious denominations in the United States and all over the world, which is affecting not only the minister but his entire family.

Chapter Four
Sources of Stress

MINISTRY CAN BE A STRESSFUL vocation. I have first-hand experience of this. Pastoral stress is a growing phenomenon in all religious denominations in the United States and all over the world, which is affecting not only the minister but his entire family. Doehring (2013) noted that "clergy are often first responders to crises experienced by people and families in their congregations and communities" (p. 623). These pastoral emergencies coupled with pastors' heavy workloads, weekly tasks of planning, preparing sermons, leading worship, and providing administrative, organizational, and educational leadership, lead to burnout.

Pastors' wives play an important role in providing support to their husbands and are impacted by the heavy responsibilities placed on them by ministry leaders. They are supposed to live an exemplary life of service to God and others in front of the congregation and the community at large (Nyabwari

& Kagema, 2014). Pastors' wives provide both support and understanding to their husbands and are inextricably linked to the ministry's success or failure (Gauger & Christie, 2013). Because of their marriage relationship, certain things are required of them to enable their pastor husbands to be successful in ministry. Furthermore, their husbands' employment demands time, and physical, mental, and emotional energy. As a result, the wives are undoubtedly affected, resulting in stress as they navigate numerous duties as wives, moms, professionals in their careers, and an additional job as a pastor's assistant (Gauger & Christie, 2013). Chan and Wong (2018) have stated that pastors' wives experience little emotional support from the church community in coping with stress from their role expectations. The church community should always be informed of issues pastors' wives are faced with and be more understanding and considerate toward their families.

Guzman and Teh (2016) observed the following stressful situations within Filipino clergy families: "difficulty of the clergy in balancing time between ministry and family, dealing with financial constraints, dealing with congregational expectations, the feeling of living in an aquarium, and the lack of external social support for the clergy wives" (p. 466). These stressful situations are not any different from those being experienced by clergy wives of Pentecostal ministers. These Filipino clergy wives also expressed difficulty finding free time for family bonding. Their husbands' on-call schedule usually posed a problem not only in their husbands being able to make time for the family but also regarding their husbands' sharing of household responsibilities with them (Guzman & Teh, 2016).

It has been observed that pastors' wives in China experienced stress from three areas, finance stress, loneliness, and role expectations (Chan & Wong, 2018). Some of the coping strategies they employed included family, social and intra-personal support (Chan & Wong, 2018). Those who had to cope with financial stress, for example, tried to be very cautious with spending money. They might engage in taking on tasks for themselves instead of paying a contractor.

I address some of these stressors in more detail below.

Role Strain. Pastors' wives have roles that might be stressful. They must care for their spouse, family, and church. Conflicting needs and priorities may make these positions stressful (Nkonge, 2020). A clergy wife may struggle to balance family and congregational commitments. Burnout may result from guilt or failure. Pastors' wives may sometimes face unreasonable expectations from their spouses and congregations. A husband may expect their wife to always offer emotional support, regardless of the time of day or other obligations. The pastor's wife may feel pressured to be a spiritual and moral role model for the church. These demands might cause burnout.

Lack of Boundaries. Pastors' wives may feel pressured to be available to the congregation and their husbands 24/7, blurring work and home life. Being always "on call" might lead to burnout. For instance, church members who need emotional assistance may contact or text a pastor's wife at any time. This makes it hard for her to relax and unwind (Jones & Plisco, 2021). The absence of work-life boundaries may also challenge pastors' wives' spiritual and emotional health. Without limits, pastors' wives may struggle to care for themselves, which can lead to burnout.

Conflict. Pastors' wives may worry about congregational or marital conflict. Leadership, theology, and interpersonal concerns may cause conflict. Conflict management may lead to burnout (Nkonge, 2020). A pastor's wife may get embroiled in a congregational dispute over an issue. She may feel pressured to arbitrate or take sides, causing tension and strain. Conflict with her husband, especially over religious work, may be complex. This might strain their relationship and affect their work.

Financial Strain. A significant number of pastors' wives do not get monetary remuneration for their labor since they do their duties in a volunteer capacity (Hutchinson, 2019). This might put the family in a difficult financial position, adding tension to their daily lives. For instance, if the husband of a clergy wife is the only earner in the family, the inability of the wife to get monetary remuneration for her labor may cause the family to experience significant financial difficulty. This may be a very trying situation for the family, especially if they are already dealing with financial issues or the pastor's spouse has a modest wage.

Isolation. Due to the demands of their responsibilities and duties, pastors' wives may feel alone. This might be worse if they serve in a new community or have few chances to socialize outside of work. A pastor's wife may feel lonely and isolated due to her duty as the spouse of the pastor, which may lead to burnout (Jones & Plisco, 2021). Moreover, pastors' wives may have little opportunity to create non-pastoral connections. This is especially difficult if they have moved, or religious work is their only social outlet. Pastors' wives may burn out if they do not have outside friends.

> Pastors and their families are, therefore, encouraged to engage in self-care and other coping strategies.

Chapter Five
Coping Strategies

THE STRESS OF MINISTRY IMPACTS the physical, spiritual, and emotional health of both the pastor and his wife. Pastors and their families are, therefore, encouraged to engage in self-care and other coping strategies.

The role of coping techniques in modulating the link between stressors, suffering, and burnout is still unknown. Pastors' wives may prevent burnout by cultivating resilience. Resilience may help manage stress and hardship. Mindfulness, self-differentiation, and Christian spiritual practices can all help deal with or prevent burnout (Frederick, *et al.*, 2018). Cognitive Behavioral Therapy (CBT), mindfulness, and social support build resilience. CBT changes negative thoughts and behavior. Pastors' spouses may improve their coping skills by working with a therapist to identify and address negative thinking patterns. The cognitive restructuring may help a pastor's wife who feels terrible about putting herself first. Acceptance and Commitment Therapy (ACT), a cognitive and behavioral therapy, has also been indicated as beneficial for all types of burnout (Montero-Marin, *et al.*, 2014).

Mindfulness, being present and accepting thoughts and emotions without judgment, may boost resilience. Mindfulness may help pastors' wives manage stress and prevent burnout. Meditation, yoga, and mindful breathing are other mindfulness practices that can be useful.

Resilience requires social support. People may feel better supported by connecting with other pastors' wives or acquaintances who understand their circumstances. Family, friends, and churchgoers provide social support (Brandon, 2022). Pastor-wife support groups can be instrumental. Social support helps mitigate occupational stress syndromes (Galek, 2011).

Systemic causes that stress pastors' wives must be addressed along with resilience. This may entail resolving inappropriate congregational expectations for pastors' wives or creating procedures to compensate for the work they do. Systemic changes may help pastors' wives avoid burnout by reducing pressures they may be faced with.

In their study, Popov, *et al.* (2013) developed The Coping Strategy Indicator, which measures three coping strategies: "problem solving, seeking social support, and avoidance" (p. 357). Popov, *et al.* (2013) described these three coping strategies:

Problem solving includes active efforts of an individual to solve the problematic situation, modify the stressful situation, or minimize its effects. Seeking support is defined as efforts to gain help and understanding of other people, as well as by seeking additional information related to the problem situation. Avoidance is a strategy that includes behavior of avoiding problematic situations either at the cognitive or behavioral level, or both (357).

Filipino clergy wives, pentecostal clergy wives, and countless others all attribute their strength and courage to prayer, spirituality, and support from family and some church members as their main coping resources (Guzman & Teh, 2016). Most of the family members, not just the wives, turn to prayer and their faith in God to cope with the stress and difficulties that they experience. Families, overall, rely on the authenticity of God's word in the reading of scriptures and offering prayers, when faced with difficult situations. Prayer serves as a means of communicating their experience with God, their frustrations, fear, joy, despair, anger, gratitude, and much more.

Support of family members is key for clergy wives who can feel isolated. Filipino families are close-knit and having the support of one another works out very well. Clergy wives can be very private and seldom have friends to confide in when going through challenges. Therefore, the family unit plays an important role for them when a situation threatens the family system. The individual personalities and coping skills of each family member are tapped as a coping resource for the family unit, and the individual resources are drawn upon to deal with that stressful situation (Guzman & Teh, 2016). Clergy wives experience little emotional support from the church community in coping with stress from their role expectations.

Self-care strategies are an accepted and expected practice within the helping professions, especially in counseling. According to Chan and Wong (2018), the psychological well-being of clergy and their spouses deserves attention for the sake of their health and the future growth of the church body. Brewster (2014) noted that "whenever a person's sense of significance is threatened by stressful encounters, it is necessary for that person to bring into action coping processes that involve new searches for significance" (p. 87).

Brewster (2014) postulated that "efforts to preserve or protect significance in the face of stressful encounters are known as 'conservational' coping methods, and people tend to turn to these as their first option in times of trouble, for example, when a clergyperson reinterprets criticisms from members of his or her congregation as opportunities to draw near to the sufferings of Jesus" (p. 87). The author went on to state that "'conservational' and 'transformational' forms of coping are complementary and interdependent mechanisms which offer individuals the possibility of equilibrium" (Brewster, 2014, p. 88).

Chapter Six
Spiritual distortions about the work of ministry

During Jesus' ministry, He performed many miracles and healings. There are some aspects of Jesus' ministry that are particularly striking. For example, He recognized the vulnerability of the sick, in their need for care. Jesus touched these people, physically and spiritually, breaking through that barrier of disease which often made people feel less than human. He touched the leper (Mark 1:41), laid hands on the blind man (Mark 8:22-25) and took the hand of the daughter of Jairus (Luke 8:54-55). His touch seemed to say to them in their wretchedness and isolation: "You are worthwhile. Through God's loving touch, you are whole. I am with you."

Second, Jesus brought the "outcast" back into human society through His healing word and touch. He challenged the notion that sickness was the result of sin. The diseased were thought of as unclean, punished by God, and cut off from

God's holy people. When His disciples asked, "Master, who did sin, this man, or his parents, that he was born blind?" (John 9:2), Jesus replied, "Neither hath this man sinned, nor his parents sinned" (John 9:3). Jesus not only touched the outcasts but welcomed them back into the community, into God's own family.

Furthermore, Jesus reaffirmed the need for spiritual healing. The paralytic lowered through the roof is first healed of his sins (Mark 2:5), while the man by the pool at Bethesda is warned, "Behold, thou art made whole: sin no more, lest a worse thing come unto thee" (John 5:14). Death itself, the ultimate affront to humanity, is overcome by Jesus. He raised Jairus' daughter (Luke 8:49-56), the widow of Nain's son (Luke 7:11-17), and Lazarus (John 11:38-44). These miracles, of course, only restored earthly life. Christ's resurrection promises believers the fullness of eternal life.

These are just a few of the many miracles Jesus performed during His time. Yet even though He was so overcome at times with people wanting to be healed or fed, He knew when to just take time to relax and regain His energy. (John 4:5-6).

God made everyone including pastors and their spouses to be managers of their lives and as such everyone must use their management skills effectively. Being in ministry and living in a world where there are endless to-do lists, managing lives can be a challenge. To manage one's life better, one needs to reprioritize one's life. One has prayerfully to determine what is important and what is not.

When Jesus heard of Lazarus' sickness and subsequent death, He stayed two more days where He was (John 11: 6). He did not leave right away. Even though Lazarus was His friend He had prayerfully to consider what to do at the time. Pastors and their spouses can follow Jesus' example here. Prioritizing issues that arise in one's life can prevent stressful

> Being in ministry and living in a world where there are endless to-do lists, managing lives can be a challenge. To manage one's life better, one needs to reprioritize one's life. One has prayerfully to determine what is important and what is not.

As hectic as Jesus' schedule was, He took time out for Himself. He often retreated from the crowds.

situations that can result in burnout. One needs to ask God in making wise decisions. As a result, one may need to let go of some or all of one's activities. One should learn the art of saying 'no.' Jesus, in the case of Lazarus said, 'not yet.' This usually tends to be a challenge for people who feel they ought to be selfless as Christians. God does not want Christians to be under constant burden or pressure, feeling obligated always to say 'yes.' God does want Christians to be a blessing to others but not at a cost that stands to jeopardize their wellbeing. So, if as a Christian you struggle with saying 'no', you should hold off making decisions until you have had time to pray and think about what God might want you do. That way, you start making Godly decisions.

As hectic as Jesus' schedule was, He took time out for Himself. He often retreated from the crowds. For example, in Mark 1: 35, Jesus took time out early in the morning to be by Himself and pray. Jesus was modeling how we as Christians should live our lives. Jesus wisely knew when to pull away after a busy period. However, in ministry, many Christians struggle to do this. And when they do, they find themselves feeling guilty because there is plenty to be done. There are so many benefits of taking time out. You get an uninterrupted opportunity to pray, rest, reflect, refocus, hear from God, be restored, refreshed and much more. Taking time out does not have to be a lengthy affair. You would be amazed what a difference a few hours or days could make when you lay aside the weight of your normal activities.

Jesus, as anointed as He was during the time of His ministry, got the support He needed and when He needed it. (Luke 8: 1-2). Pastors and their spouses at times try to fulfill a huge calling or task by themselves, sometimes because of the fear of betrayal of trust. They are unsure of who to trust even amongst their parishioners. A support mechanism is always helpful

...AS WE GLANCE THROUGH THE BIBLE, WE NOTICE THAT MANY GREAT LEADERS HAD SUPPORT OF SOME KIND.

...JESUS HAD HIS DISCIPLES; DAVID HAD HIS MIGHTY MEN OF VALOR

because it becomes increasingly important the greater the responsibility of the ministry gets. When adequate support is lacking, there is usually trouble ahead. Ministers of God who start off on a high, sooner or later, find themselves depleted of every kind of resource (physical, spiritual, financial, etc.) Yet, as we glance through the Bible, we notice that many great leaders had support of some kind. For example, Jesus had His disciples; David had his mighty men of valor (1 Chronicles 12:51). The 'supporters' were there to help their leaders in more ways than one. Whether you have a ministry or some huge responsibility, you can still surround yourself with godly people who can be of support to you on this journey called life.

God rested on the Sabbath, and He commanded His people to do the same. Ministers of God can use the day they regard as Sabbath to rest after the usual service. There are pastors who even after a busy week still use the afternoons on Sundays to do home and hospital visitations. They want to use this day to catch up on unfinished tasks. The problem here is that they do not get a chance to take their hands off the steering wheel. God has given a formula to aid ministers and even their spouses in living an abundant, healthy, and balanced life. Accordingly, they should choose to enjoy their God-given day of rest regardless of the pressures around them.

As we have discovered, having to fulfill some of the unrealistic expectations in the church and even at home, pastors' wives suffer from burnout. Our Lord and Savior Jesus seemed to know how to deal with some of the stressors with which He was faced. He took time away to rest and even encouraged His disciples to do so. (Mark 6: 31-32). Pastors' wives in ministry should take the time to rest likewise. The next chapter highlights recommendations for pastors' wives to prevent and cope with burnout.

> Churches need to take some responsibility for the wellbeing of pastors' wives.

Chapter Seven
Recommendations

As I have discussed, burnout occurs slowly, but once it has set in, it is usually challenging to counter. Accordingly, it is essential to be cognizant of its early signs and actively work on ways to prevent it.

Churches need to take some responsibility for the well-being of pastors' wives. Churches should reevaluate their expectations of clergy spouses and allow them to participate in decision-making. It is recommended that clergy wives be acknowledged, encouraged, and given the authority to lead and minister alongside their husbands.

In encouraging their pastors' wives, churches should not place unrealistic expectations on them. The pastor's wife's time with her family should be respected. The Church must be willing to support and help ease the load of the pastor and his wife. The Church should pray for the pastor's wife and her family as they are the backbone of the ministry and in the frontline of all affairs within the ministry. Church leaders and pastors should also educate their members regarding the impact that their behavior (either good or bad) can have on clergy families.

It is also recommended that pastors' wives begin to communicate and be open to share their concerns in ministry. Having appropriate support structures in place is very crucial for pastors' wives. Establishing reliable support structures for them will assist in helping them break their mode of silence over issues affecting them in ministry. Pastoral couples should give insight into what is needed to help their well-being and their overall success in ministry, especially pastors' wives who suffer in silence. To help ease their suffering, clinical professionals, pastoral or spiritual counselors, chaplains, psychologists, and other professional practitioners whose role is to care for pastors' wives, should help establish such structures. Counselors and ministers should not disregard clergy spouses' history, roles, and positions due to the nature of their jobs. Pastors' wives also need to find reliable mentors. Good friends, supportive relationships, family, and peers can sustain them as they continue in their roles as pastors' wives.

Churches, district leaders, and denominational heads should consider the expense of offering counseling to pastoral families. Churches should equip clergy spouses with material and financial tools to help them manage stress and avoid burnout. Offering them seminars on stress management and burnout prevention is ideal.

To alleviate any financial stress on the pastor and his wife, members of the trustee board, or deacons appointed to handle the finances of the church, should be the ones ensuring that all bills of the ministry are paid. The pastor and his wife should not be the ones to handle the church's financial needs since that can cause financial and personal strain on them. Churches should be able to come up with ways to mitigate the financial issues that churches tend to face.

> Pastoral couples should give insight into what is needed to help their well-being and their overall success in ministry, especially pastors' wives who suffer in silence.

Chapter Eight
Conclusion

Burnout can occur when one feels overwhelmed and unable to meet constant demands. The literature and research on burnout uncover that it usually leads to unhappiness which can eventually threaten one's job, relationships, and health (mental, emotional, physical, and spiritual) and that it often occurs among individuals in the helping professions. Burnout is a widespread problem in many careers, including pastoral (Frederick, *et al.*, 2018). It is more than the occasional overload at work.

Pastors' wives have experienced burnout as they serve alongside their pastor husbands. Sometimes at the expense of their well-being, clergy members are charged with giving emotional and spiritual support to their congregations. Unfortunately, their spouses' experiences have been largely neglected. Many have been suffering in silence, and their situations tend to worsen since they are mostly ignored and understudied. Many clergy wives are not prepared for the demands of holding their positions. Some were not called into ministry; they only found themselves as the pastor's wife when their husband became a pastor after marriage. However, some who knew what they were getting themselves into by being the pastor's wife still suffered burnout despite their knowledge. Burnout can result from the many responsibilities pastors' wives have to carry.

The Church needs to acknowledge the position of the pastor's wife. Instead of silencing pastors' wives and limiting their free will, the Church needs to acknowledge them and allow them to participate in the Church's decision-making. Clergy wives should be well taken care of.

The clergy wife sacrifices a lot to minister alongside her husband. It is easy for her to get overwhelmed by this unwieldy position, considering that she also has a family and a husband to take care of. Those who are also career women may need to work both day and night to fulfill their church and home duties (Jones & Plisco, 2021).

Pastors need the time to spend with their wives to prevent or reduce loneliness and consequent burnout. As much as pastors need to minister to their sometime many members, they also need to dedicate enough time to their wives. For instance, sometimes clergy may receive and need to attend to stress calls from their members in the middle of the night, leaving their wives alone. Some pastors' wives may experience long weeks of being without their husbands who are away doing ministry work. Some pastors may need lengthy alone time for sermon preparation and prayer. Hence, many pastors' wives spend little time with their mates which can result in loneliness.

High expectations placed on pastors' wives by the church and its members may result in stress among pastors' wives, and since many of them do not have confidants they can trust, the situation may lead to burnout. Pastors' wives are often not expected to show weakness, attending church even if they have health issues. In addition, society often expects the children of pastors to be exactly like their fathers and that it is the role of the pastors' wives to make that happen in their husbands' absence. Moreover, pastors' wives may be expected to fill in any gaps in the church's ministry and end up with responsibilities that they did not bargain for. These expectations create much pressure on them, resulting in stress.

Pastors' wives should be educated or educate themselves, by reading books, for example, about the journey they have chosen to follow, whether or not they are planning to be active in their husband's ministry or in theirs. They should learn in advance about the obstacles they will face during their line of work and especially how to handle stress and deal with lonely days in ministry. In addition, pastors' wives need mentors to guide them through some of the expectations associated with being a pastor's wife and how to deal with situations that may result in burnout.

For pastors' wives to be free from burnout, they need to eradicate its symptoms as soon as they appear. They must work to eliminate stressors at home and in ministry. They need to involve themselves in activities that are likely to keep them adjusted. In addition, turning to God through prayer can help in the reduction of stress. The mental health of pastors' wives matters, and it is important to deal with stress before things get out of hand. Also, talking things out at home is a way of curbing stressors.

Pastors' wives are important personnel in the ministry and should be assisted and taken care of to prevent them from experiencing burnout. They need to be heard. They have been silent for too long. Many pastors' wives simply yearn for those who can give them a listening ear and not be critical or judgmental of them–someone they can pour out their feelings to with no fear of condemnation or worry that they will experience retaliation. They long for a safe place to vent their frustrations and feel loved and accepted just as they are. They long for grace-based members of Christ's body to reach out to them and make a difference in their personal lives so that they can go back into their local church situation with renewed hope and joy. In the United States and around the world this need is being met by a growing number of ministries whose aim is to help the spiritually tired and wounded. Various kinds of retreats are available to help ministry families prevent burnout before it occurs. In a resource article[4], the pastor's wife is encouraged to establish her own bill of rights[5]. The key to living in joy as part of her spouse's ministry is to focus on who she is and her ability to function effectively. However, churches also can help develop programs, as I recommended in the previous chapter.

We, the wives of pastors, must keep speaking out so that other women may realize that being called to ministry does not mean being called to silence our struggles and pain.

---

4   Focus on the Family. www.family.org
5   See Appendix A for an example.

> We, the wives of pastors, must keep speaking out so that other women may realize that being called to ministry does not mean being called to silence our struggles and pain.

Appendix A

A Poem for the Pastor's Wife[6]

The Pastor's Wife

She's a Godly woman, she has such grace
Always a warm greeting, a smile on her face
She's always encouraging, **she knows her place**
She is - The Pastor's Wife.

She has to always look just right
Always on time, though the schedule's tight
From early morning, 'til late at night
Always - The Pastor's Wife.

She's such a Lady, everyone's friend
She serves with love from deep within
All the rifts she tries to mend
Oh she's - The Pastor's Wife.

She carries your burdens, she prays for you
Sometimes she cries the whole night through

---

6   A Poem for the Pastor's Wife. Judy Bowling (2014, January 30). WordPress. https://umcdea.wordpress.com/2014/01/30/the-pastors-wife/

But you won't know when she's feeling blue
'Cause she's - The Pastor's Wife.

At church as she starts to walk up the aisle
So many need to stop and talk for awhile
Though she is tired, she has her own trials
She's patient, she's - The Pastor's Wife.

Her life, her time, is not her own
There's always a need, they go on and on
With a knock at the door, or a ringing phone
That's the life of - The Pastor's Wife.

Her husband she shares with a whole congregation
She humbly accepts his intense dedication
In loneliness she kneels to see consolation
God Bless - The Pastor's Wife.

She will someday reach the end of this race
As she meets her Master face to face
Surely our God has a Special Place
In Heaven for - The Pastor's Wife.

A Bill of Rights for the Pastor's Wife[7]

Try being yourself. Resist letting your spouse, children, or church family push you to become someone you don't want to be. Use your best gifts most often. Do the things you do the best and delegate what you don't do well - and don't feel guilty about it.

Make your priorities obvious. Let the congregation know what's important to you. Don't let the church squeeze you into their mold, and don't overreact so they think you are too good to be a servant. A delicate balance is needed.

Don't attempt to control the church. Work alongside people in your church. Be a happy affirming helper rather than the one who has all the answers and influences all the decisions.

Listen more and talk less. You help others the most when you just listen. Do not condemn or put people in their place. Listen and allow others to come to their own conclusions about issues of consequence.

---

7   London, H. R. & Wiseman, N. B. 2003, (August 25). Married To A Pastor's Wife. Crosswalk. https://www.crosswalk.com/church/pastors-or-leadership/a-bill-of-rights-for-a-pastors-spouse-560640.html

Show visible love to your spouse. In your conversations let people know that your spouse is both special and human. Keep showing the church that you love one another and you care for each other.

Talk about advantages to your children. Never tell your children they have to do something because they are the pastor's children. Give better reasons for your family standard – there are many. Don't expect perfection, but help them know that while they have demands, they also have privileges. Help them see how they have a positive part in your family's shared ministry.

Find a prayer partner as a soul mate. Seek to be part of, or even establish, a clergy-spouse group to hold each other accountable. Be honest with one another.

Take a worship break. Go somewhere every few months where you can worship as a family. Find someone, other than your spouse, who can be your pastor.

Don't spiritualize everything. Enjoy life – its ups and downs – without becoming so religious in your outlook that you're no fun to be around. Learn to laugh at yourself and your situation. Have a life outside of church activities.

Schedule vacation days and date nights. See to it that your spouse puts important family dates on the calendar.

Encourage your spouse to find an accountability partner. Every pastor needs a covenant partner, where "pastoral stuff" can be talked about and burdens understood and shared.

SOLACE

Don't bug your spouse. Everyone knows the heavy demands on pastors - they don't need to be reminded all the time. However, never let your spouse off the hook where you and the kids are concerned. Your home and your marriage energize and stabilize his or her ministry.

Stay attentive to your spouse's needs. Don't back away. There will be times when your spouse, under the weight of the struggle, will become sullen, aloof, and depressed. This is when he or she needs you the most. Try doubling or tripling your affection and support.

Commit to self-care. Take care of yourself - spiritually, emotionally, and physically. Continue to mature spiritually.

Bibliography

Andor, J. (2013). The role of the pastor's wife in ministry. AAMM, 8, 21-35. ResearchGate. https://www.researchgate.net/publication/283495905

Armstrong, N. (2013). 'I Insisted I Was Myself': clergy wives and authentic selfhood in England c. 1960-94. Women's History Review, 22(6), 995-1013. https://doi.org/10.1080/09612025.2013.780842[8]

Ash, R. V. (2011). The problems facing a pastor's wife today. WLQ: 81(1), 1-18. http://www.wlsessays.net/bitstream/handle/123456789/164/AshWife

Aulthouse, M. E. "Clergy families: The helpless forgottens' cry for help answered through reality therapy." *Vistas Online* 47 (2013): 20-24.

Beeke, J. R. (2013). The minister's helpmeet. *Puritan Reformed Journal*, 5(2), 209-218.

---

[8] Where no website address is provided, links are taken from Liberty University's database of articles.

Brandon, G. Q. (2022). Preaching through Desensitized Emotions: Clergy Burnout in the African American Church (Doctoral dissertation, Virginia Union University).

Brewster, C. (2014). Religious coping among rural clergy: Measuring ways in which rural clergy draw on coping strategies informed by their theological beliefs. *Journal of Empirical Theology*, 27(1), 85–102. https://doi.org/10.1163/15709256-12341297

Chan, K., & Chen, M. (2019). Experience of stress and burnout among pastors in China. *The Journal of Pastoral Care & Counseling*: JPCC, 73(4), 232–237. https://doi.org/10.1177/1542305019886533

Chan, K., & Wong, M. (2018). Experience of stress and coping strategies among pastors' wives in China. *The Journal of Pastoral Care & Counseling: JPCC*, 72(3), 163–171. https://doi.org/10.1177/1542305018782518

Comiskey, S. E. (2022). Helping Missionaries Build Effective Ministry Marriage Practice: A Video Series Designed to Equip Victory Family Centre Missionaries Worldwide. Dissertation. Assemblies of God Theological Seminary.

Doehring, C. (2013). New directions for clergy experiencing stress: Connecting spirit and body. *Pastoral Psychology*, 62(5), 623–638. https://doi.org/10.1007/s11089-013-0512-1

Drumm, R., Cooper, L., Seifert, M., McBride, D., & Sedlacek, D. (2017). "Love everybody, keep your mouth shut, don't have an opinion": Role expectations among Seventh-Day Adventist pastor spouses. *Social Work & Christianity*, 44(3), 94–114.

Francis, L. J., Robbins, M., & Wulff, K. (2013). Are clergy serving yoked congregations more vulnerable to burnout? A study among clergy serving in the Presbyterian church (U.S.A.). Stress and Health: *Journal of the International Society for the Investigation of Stress*, 29(2), 113–116. https://doi.org/10.1002/smi.2434

Freudenberger, H. J. (1974). Staff Burnout. Journal of Social Issues. Wiley

Frederick, T. V., Dunbar, S., & Thai, Y. (2018). Burnout in Christian perspective. *Pastoral Psychology, 67*(3), 267–276. https://doi.org/10.1007/s11089-017-0799-4

Galek, K., Flannelly, K., Greene, P., & Kudler, T. (2011). Burnout, secondary traumatic stress, and social support. *Pastoral Psychology, 60*(5), 633–649. https://doi.org/10.1007/s11089-011-0346-7

Gauger, R. & Christie, L. (2013). Clergy stress and depression. Retrieved on 2nd February 2017 https://www.pdresources.org/uploads/course/f1b78.pdf

Guzman, N., & Teh, L. (2016). Understanding the stresses and coping resources of Filipino clergy families: A multiple-case study. *Pastoral Psychology*, 65(4), 459-480. https://doi.org/10.1007/s11089-016-0698-0

Hester, J. A (2018). "Stress and longevity in pastoral ministry: A phenomenological study."

Hoffert, S. D. (2019). Anna Burwell and the business of being a Presbyterian minister's wife in North Carolina, 1835-1857. *North Carolina Historical Review, 96*(3), 245–275.

Hutchinson, D. K. M. (2019). African American Female Clergy in Dual Clergy Marriage (Doctoral dissertation, Walden University).

Jones, L., & Plisco, M. (2021). The stories of women, by women, married to male ministry leaders. Mental Health, Religion & Culture, 24(10), 1037-1049.

Langberg, D. (1988). Counsel for Pastors' Wives. Grand Rapids: Ministry Resources Library.

Lane, B. (2012 – 2022). https://expastors.com/7-ways-pastors-can-stay-encouraged-and-healthy-in-ministry/

Litchfield, D. H. (2016). ed. *Classified List of 4800 Serials: Currently Received in the Libraries of the University of Pennsylvania and of Bryn Mawr, Haverford, and Swarthmore Colleges.* University of Pennsylvania Press.

Luedtke, A. C., & Sneed, K. J. (2018). Voice of the clergy wife: A phenomenological study. The Journal of Pastoral Care & Counseling: JPCC, 72(1), 63–72. https://doi.org/10.1177/1542305018762212

Miller, D. (2009). What is the Role of the Pastor's Wife Part 2. Retrieved from https://sharperiron.org/article/what-role-of-pastors-wife-part-2

Montero-Marin, J., Prado-Abril, J., Piva Demarzo, M. M., Gascon, S., & García-Campayo, J. (2014). Coping with stress and types of burnout: Explanatory power of different coping strategies. *PLoS ONE*, *9*(2), 1–9. https://doi.org/10.1371/journal.pone.0089090

Nandasaba, T. L. (2011). Determination of effects of stress to Pastors' wives on church ministries performance: A case of Bungoma South District.

Nkonge, G. (2020). The influence of pastoral church leadership on the behavior of pastors' children: a case study of east Africa Pentecostal churches in Meru county (Doctoral dissertation, Pan Africa Christian University).

Nyabwari, B. G. & Kagema, D. N. (2014). "Charismatic Pentecostal Churches in Kenya: Growth, Culture and Orality." *International Journal of Humanities Social Sciences and Education (IJHSSE)*.

Popov, B., Miljanović, M., Stojaković, M., & Matanović, J. (2013). Work stressors, distress, and burnout: The role of coping strategies. *Primenjena Psihologija*, *6*(4), 355–370.

Acknowledgements

I WANT TO ACKNOWLEDGE THE PRESENCE of the Holy Spirit, who has always been my guide. It was because of His leading that the title of my dissertation was birthed and has now culminated to the writing of this book, aimed to be a source of enlightenment to pastors, their spouses, the church and her leaders, helping professionals, and other stakeholders. Thank you, Holy Spirit, for also upholding me and bestowing your grace on me when I was faced with burnout. To God be the glory!

Many thanks to my mother, Madam Patricia Wyse (now deceased), who was there to help with the children as I juggled work, school, ministry, and the home front.

I also want to acknowledge my late maternal grandmother, Madam Elizabeth T. Cole, who selflessly served numerous pastors in her days and gave birth to sons who later became pastors themselves, and who through her lineage, many more pastors and pastors' wives have been birthed.

My sincere thanks and appreciation to Morenike Euba Oyenusi for painstakingly putting this book together; may the Lord reward you for all you do.

About the Author

Dr. Patricia Aladekoba is an ordained reverend and the Vice-President of Christ Throne Ministries which she co-pastors with her husband. She holds a Bachelor of Arts degree in French, Latin, and Linguistics. She also holds a Master of Business Administration, a Master of Arts in Pastoral Counseling and Spiritual Guidance, and a Doctorate in Education, Community Care & Counseling. She is a certified Temperament Counselor as well as a Substance Abuse Counselor. She is a certified Professional Clinical Member of the National Christian Counselors Association and a certified Pastoral Member of the Sarasota Academy of Christian Counseling.

Dr. Aladekoba loves to dance, cook, sing, and watch movies, in her spare time. She looks forward to climbing the Eiffel Tower one day. She is married to Apostle (Dr.) Anthony Aladekoba, and they are blessed with wonderful children.

www.ingramcontent.com/pod-product-compliance
Lightning Source LLC
Chambersburg PA
CBHW051617010526
44107CB00043B/1494/J